Love, Passion, And Betrayal

Love, Passion, And Betrayal

BOOK OF POEMS

BRITTANI NECHELLE DARENSBOURG

Contents

Introduction/ About The Author

"I fell in love with poetry at the age of 9 years old. In third grade, I won first place in the Young Author's Contest at Carver Elementary School in Hahnville, LA when I wrote my first book of poems. Writing on paper what's inside my heart is a blessing to me. Poetry is very special to me because it's more than just reading it, you also can feel it. I'm so blessed and grateful for the world to finally be able to see my work. Thank you, Jesus."

-Brittani Darensbourg

Author

PART ONE

Love

Love

Expressing passionate thoughts from the heart, like a piece of art. The love is so strong I don't know where to start. Imaginations flow through my mind all the time, it's so easy to believe you're mine. By looking into your eyes, I see the same signs. A mutual connection receiving the same affection. Two souls bond together, I know this love will last forever. Showing amazing feelings that comes from the heart, true love never falls apart.

By: Brittani Darensbourg

The One

As the sunset approaches, I notice a mortal coming closer to me. I was thinking maybe this could be the one who sets me free. Slowly approaching each other closer, I glanced into his exotic eyes as he stared into mines, I imagine my hands tracing the pattern of his strong, healthy arms and hoping he thought of me as a charm. Burning desires arise in my heart, wishing that this moment won't ever fall apart. Fantasies of his warm gentle touch, I never will think of this as too much. Curious as of what has begun, but this moment tells me you're.......The One.

By: Brittani Darensbourg

The Stranger On The Bayou

Mesmerized by his clear non-native eyes, enraptured by his glowing, toned biceps, slowly running hands through his hair as the color of sand, he turns to look my way. The view of him just takes my breath away. As we stare eye to eye, the connection arises, telling me he is all I needed to find. Just as the waves came in rush, I yearn for you much more than a crush. Daydreams of being closer to you, who is the stranger on the bayou

By: Brittani Darensbourg

Candlelight

Heat waves raise as the daylight fades. Slow burning, smoke just as rare with so much romance in the air. The look in your eyes, I can't deny, what we feel is so so real. Only time will tell if this love is just a fairytale. Candlelight shines bright all during this starry night. Reflection of your affection, makes me feel a strong attraction. Nothing else amounts to this satisfaction. Tonight is set so right, with smooth burning... Candlelight.

By: Brittani Darensbourg

Always And Forever

Moments with you are neither sad nor too soon. Exciting emotions develop making my whole heart bloom. Your pure kind touch means so much making my mind shoot to the moon. As opposites attract, getting so attached, this is always and forever. To give you all my love, I surrender. Through the good times and the bad times, you're mine. This love is one of a kind... Always and forever.

By: Brittani Darensbourg

What I See

Water perfectly reflects, as the sunset. The wind blows at the moment daylight slowly goes, my eyes rise when looking in the sky. In my mind, this view is one of a kind. What I see, makes me believe its beauty indeed. An exotic view so true, makes life feel brand new. Soothe feeling of relief is all because of what I see.

By: Brittani Darensbourg

Attraction

Giving my eyes all the satisfaction makes me want nothing but affection. I fantasize of your handsome face, having my heart beating at a faster pace. Your smile so perfect I can see it from a mile. Your clear green eyes caught my attention by surprise. Thinking of your soft-looking healthy skin, makes me grin, knowing I'm guilty as sin. I'm hoping this sight of you never end. Just like two souls get attached, opposites attract.

By: Brittani Darensbourg

The Boy Across The Way

An open window gives me a perfect view. Making it hard to believe that is true. His clear tanned skin glows just as the sun arose. Hair dark as night with a smile that's so bright. Eye to eye for a moment we stare. I catch myself fantasizing about future memories we can make and share. As the day fades away in my heart lounging for these feelings to stay. Deep down knowing this short-term love will leave and go astray. Informing myself that I am infatuated with the boy across the way.

By: Brittani Darensbourg

PART TWO

Passion

Passion

Causalities of love full of strong emotion. My soul craves so much for your gentle touch. This intense feeling has my heart healing. I know for sure, that this feeling is pure. As time passes I hope this love last. True passion doesn't go away fast. You don't have a clue the feeling of you sticks to me like glue. It's so hard to resist you. Just about anything. I'll do to prove to you my passion is real and true.

By: Brittani Darensbourg

Silk Stalkings

Through my bedroom window, I see evening sunset rays just above the satin waves. Palm trees whisper in the summer eve breeze. As the night moves in, love sets within. I turned to look away, there you were, standing in my doorway. Walking closer to me, I naturally feel the heat. Silk stalkings increasing steamy desires, only he admires. Giving him kisses that he misses, he moves his hands, on silk stalkings where they land. Gliding his fingertips across my hips, silk stalkings making it hard to grip. He looks into my eyes as his arms tire, I've realized silk stalkings be his true desire.

By: Brittani Darensbourg

Dark Desire

Dark desire burns light as flames of fire. Passion flows through the air, like a love affair. A mutual connection makes this very moment so fair. Dark desires fulfilling love and care. Tender love, pulling you closer as I stare. Erotic feelings flowing through the air. This action called passion, giving me all the satisfaction. I crave so much of you. Feelings that I have is all so true. As reality hits in a bother, this is only a dark desire.

By: Brittani Darensbourg

Whispers In The Dark

The closer you appear, I feel you near. Held tight through the night, as we rest, our skin caress. Whispering seductive words I've never heard. I feel the sensation of a soft breath coming upon my ear but no shadow appears. Room black as night makes the mood so right. Hard to see, but I know you it'll be. Running fingers through my hair, having the presence of you is just so fair. So amazed by erotic soft thoughts, my brain sparks when hearing whispers in the dark

By: Brittani Darensbourg

Fantasies

I always dream of you. Every day, it gets more exciting and new. In the moment I smile knowing my feelings are true about you. All the time this fantasy is on my mind. I hope one day you feel the same way and be mine. Together forever even through stormy weather. Through thick and thin this emotion won't ever end. I continue to feel the same all over again. I realize I just fantasize that this desire is so alive. Hoping its more than what the eyes can see instead of being all one lovely fantasy.

By: Brittani Darensbourg

PART THREE

Betrayal

Ultimate Betrayal

I talk you don't listen, sitting here wondering what's wrong and what's missing. Days go by as the time fly, I've noticed you throw my feelings to the side. Your love has gone away so much, no sensitivity or gentleness to your touch. Day by day this situation is hard for me to face. Knowledge of knowing we are departing makes my heart beat at a faster pace. My emotions come to fear when you are not near. Every day my mind tells me one day you're going to disappear. I never thought I would get mistreated, the false love you gave me was very misleaded. Our love story has gone down the road to fatal. This is my lesson of ultimate betrayal.

By: Brittani Darensbourg

Temptations

Heart full of lust, the look in your eyes I'm unable to describe. Being alone makes me think otherwise, but being with you, I don't need to rush. The smile you give me always makes me blush. Signs and signals I receive tell me this is a game of deceit.

Moments that I've recapped confirm I'm falling into a deadly trap. Snares is the only thing you have to share. All the characteristics of you are just so rare. This vibe you and I have is hard to explain but can't no longer be entertained. I choose not to fall into temptation, it burns forever.

By: Brittani Darensbourg

Flirting With Danger

Bare skin with a grin, the look in your eyes just guilty as sin. Silky hairs flow with the wind. The sight of you my heart won't let my eyes hide. The feeling of knowing that you are filled with lies. A fling that will be filled up with deceive, I will receive. A love game of cat and mouse in your plan to achieve. A moment of pleasure that will leave me with anger. The signs of flirting with danger.

By: Brittani Darensbourg

Sleeping with my Enemy

False affection with fading attraction. As time passes, I feel there's no more true satisfaction. Anger develops in my heart. You feel like a total stranger. They say true love lasts forever but I always seem to question why are we still together. Our home is just so cold. Being with you is really getting old. The good doesn't out way the bad which makes me feel so sad. The betrayal you gave me, this love is no longer a fairytale. To each other, we are not friendlily. I have come to terms that I'm sleeping with my enemy

By: Brittani Darensbourg

The Failing Of Love

So much in love with you that it fills my heart. Millions of emotions to express; I don't know where to start. Knowing that our feelings are not mutual is the most hurtful part.

Gathered thoughts of being sentimental increasing my mind to wonder and fall apart. We rose in the beginning yet now going into a terrible ending. I never thought a powerful thing called love could be so distant between two people. You and I both know that our bond was never equal. I always thought we fit each other like a glove. We are at the end of the tunnel, something called..... The failing of love.

By: Brittani Darensbourg

Til Lies Do Us Part

Being with you for years, I never thought I'd cry so many tears. All this time, you gave me false love to keep me near. My heart shatters and breaks. It's so hard to get over, I don't know how much more I can take. You have shown me no signs of care. Myself has reached up to a point of more than I can bare. From the beginning, I was treated so unfairly. This feels so rare, so many lies you told me I don't know where to start. It's time for me to leave and play it smart.....Til lies do us part.

By: Brittani Darensbourg

A Lover's Revenge

So much pain inside my heart, It seems to tear me apart. Many things to explain, and I don't know where to start. The dirt I was served I didn't deserve. I hope one day you realize you will have to pay. No matter what you do, you can't play it safe. Although this is very hard, in the end, I will get the reward. In due time, you will realize I am the prize. For years you fed me lies that I despise and taken by surprise. Usually, I don't seek revenge. This is speaking from the heart of a lover's revenge.

By: Brittani Darensbourg